LECTURE NO. 4, CODES AND CIPHERS OF THE CIVIL WAR

WILLIAM F. *FRIEDMAN*

Solve me:

QDOJHQ FRPPHQGHG

WKH SHRSOH RI

WKH ZLWK

Hint for the reader: patriots and tiki torches FTW.

NIMBLE BOOKS LLC: THE AI LAB FOR BOOK-LOVERS

~ FRED ZIMMERMAN, EDITOR ~

Humans and AI making books richer, more diverse, and more surprising.

PUBLISHING INFORMATION

(c) 2024 Nimble Books LLC
ISBN: 978-1-60888-303-5

AI-GENERATED KEYWORD PHRASES

Telegraph Corps; cryptosystems; Federal Signal Corps; Confederate Signal Corps; Military Telegraph Corps; cipher book; code equivalents; enciphered messages; key terms; plain-text messages; cipher table; message encryption; Civil War communication; historical cryptography; military communication.

PUBLISHER'S NOTES

This annotated edition illustrates the capabilities of the AI Lab for Book-Lovers to add context and ease-of-use to manuscripts. It includes several types of abstracts, building from simplest to more complex: TLDR (one word), ELI5, TLDR (vanilla), Scientific Style, and Action Items; essays to increase viewpoint diversity, such as Grounds for Dissent, Red Team Critique, and MAGA Perspective; and Notable Passages and Nutshell Summaries for each page.

ANNOTATIONS

This lecture provides a fascinating glimpse into the world of cryptology during the American Civil War, highlighting the systems used by both Union and Confederate forces, as well as the challenges and rivalries that existed.[1]

Key Points:

- **Albert J. Myer and the Signal Corps:** The lecture details Myer's development of the "wig-wag" system of visual signaling and the subsequent establishment of the Signal Corps. The initial lack of electrical telegraphy capabilities and the ensuing rivalry with the U.S. Military Telegraph Corps (USMTC) created significant challenges for the Signal Corps.

- **Union Cryptosystems:** The lecture describes the two primary cryptosystems used by the Union:

    - **Myer's Cipher Disk**: Employed by the Signal Corps for tactical communications, this disk allowed for changing the visual signal equivalents for letters, offering a basic level of encryption.

    - Route Ciphers: Utilized by the USMTC for strategic communications, these ciphers involved transposing words within a matrix, offering a more complex level of encryption compared to the Myer disk.

- **Confederate Cryptosystems:** The lecture explains the Confederate reliance on the Vigenère cipher, also known as the "court cipher," for both tactical and strategic communications. This system used a keyword to shift alphabets cyclically, providing a polyalphabetic encryption method.

- **Weaknesses of the Systems:** The lecture critically examines the weaknesses of both Union and Confederate cryptosystems:

---

[1] The AI did a good job on this summary, but it should have mentioned one important point extrinsic to the document: the author of these lectures, William Friedman, was the founding father of American cryptography.

- **Myer's Cipher Disk:** Susceptible to cryptanalysis due to its monoalphabetic nature.

- **Route Ciphers:** Vulnerable if codebooks were captured, and the limited number of code words reduced their effectiveness.

- **Confederate Vigenère Ciphers:** Leaving words unenciphered and revealing word lengths through the cipher text compromised security. Additionally, the limited number of keys used during the war made them susceptible to cryptanalysis.

Additional Observations:

- The lecture highlights the importance of cryptology in warfare, emphasizing its role in secure communication and the impact of insecure communications on the outcome of battles and campaigns.

- It reveals the lack of advanced cryptographic knowledge during the Civil War era, with both sides relying on relatively simple systems that were often vulnerable to cryptanalysis.

- The lecture raises interesting questions about the effectiveness of the Union and Confederate cryptosystems and the potential impact of their weaknesses on the course of the war.

Further Exploration:

- Investigate the historical accounts of specific battles or campaigns where intercepted communications played a significant role.

- Explore the development of cryptology after the Civil War and compare the systems used in later conflicts.

- Research the life and contributions of Albert J. Myer and other key figures in the history of cryptology.

Overall, the lecture provides a valuable introduction to the fascinating world of Civil War cryptology and offers insights into the evolution of secure communications in warfare.

Fred Zimmerman using Google Gemini 1.5

ABSTRACTS

TL;DR (ONE WORD)

Cipher.

EXPLAIN IT TO ME LIKE I'M FIVE YEARS OLD

The document discusses the cryptosystems used by the Federal Signal Corps and the Confederate Signal Corps. It mentions a message enciphered in Cipher Book No. 4 and the use of key terms like "Manchester Bluff" and "Complete Victory" to encode messages. The document also talks about the distribution of copies of the cipher book among members of the Military Telegraph Corps in different states. Additionally, it mentions the words used as code equivalents in the messages. This indicates that the document is focused on

TL;DR (VANILLA)

The document discusses the cryptosystems used by the Federal Signal Corps and the Confederate Signal Corps. It mentions the distribution of a specific document within the Military Telegraph Corps and the use of certain words as code equivalents in messages. It also provides examples of messages enciphered using specific key terms.

SCIENTIFIC STYLE

The document appears to discuss the cryptosystems used by the Federal Signal Corps and the Confederate Signal Corps during the Civil War. It mentions the distribution of certain documents to members of the Military Telegraph Corps in different states. Additionally, it references the use of code equivalents and enciphering messages using specific key terms. The content seems to focus on the transmission of secure messages during the wartime period.

ACTION ITEMS

The document appears to be discussing the cryptosystems used by the Federal Signal Corps and the Confederate Signal Corps during the Civil War.

It mentions specific cipher books used by the Telegraph Corps and the distribution of these books among different states.

The document also includes examples of messages that were enciphered using specific key terms.

The mention of code equivalents and plain-text messages indicates a focus on encryption and decryption methods used during the time period.

Based on these sentences, it seems that the document provides a detailed analysis of the communication methods and encryption techniques used by the Signal Corps during the Civil War

VIEWPOINTS

These perspectives increase the reader's exposure to viewpoint diversity.

GROUNDS FOR DISSENT

A member of the organization responsible for this document might have principled, substantive reasons to dissent from this report for several reasons.

Firstly, the document appears to contain nonsensical and disjointed sentences that do not seem to have any relevance or coherence to the topic at hand. This could lead a member to question the credibility and reliability of the information presented in the report.

Additionally, the mention of cryptosystems used by both the Federal Signal Corps and the Confederate Signal Corps could be a sensitive topic for some members, especially if they have strong opinions or affiliations with either side. This could lead to concerns about bias or impartiality in the report's analysis.

Furthermore, the mention of specific individuals and locations in a seemingly random and disconnected manner could raise privacy or security concerns for some members. They may feel uncomfortable with the level of detail provided in the report and question the appropriateness of disclosing such information.

Overall, a member of the organization responsible for this document may have legitimate reasons to dissent from the report based on its lack of coherence, potential biases, and privacy implications.

RED TEAM CRITIQUE

The document appears to discuss cryptosystems used by both the Federal Signal Corps and the Confederate Signal Corps. However, the selected sentences are fragmented and do not provide a clear and coherent overview of the content. The inclusion of nonsensical phrases and unrelated words such as "Madison square Brown" and "rustle silk" suggests that there may be errors or inaccuracies in the text. Additionally, the mention of cipher books and key terms for enciphering messages indicates a focus on encryption methods. The lack of context and organization in the extracted sentences makes it difficult to fully understand the purpose and significance of the document. Overall, the document may require editing and reorganization to improve clarity and coherence.

MAGA PERSPECTIVE

This document is a mess of jumbled nonsense, clearly written by someone with no grasp of coherent language. It's no wonder the Telegraph Corps had trouble deciphering anything with the garbled words and strange phrases used. The fact that they are even discussing cryptosystems is laughable, considering how disorganized and unclear their communication already is. It's no surprise that the Confederate Signal Corps struggled to communicate effectively when their counterparts were producing such incomprehensible garbage.

The mention of different codes and cipher books just highlights the inefficiency and incompetence of the Federal Signal Corps. It's no wonder they had to send out so many copies to different states, as no one could possibly decipher the messages without the key terms. The fact that they used terms like "Manchester Bluff" and "Complete Victory" as keys just shows how amateurish and unprofessional their encryption methods were.

It's no wonder they had trouble in their operations, with such haphazard and ineffective communication strategies.

The sheer lack of clarity and coherence in this document is concerning. It's filled with random words and phrases thrown together with no apparent rhyme or reason. This is not how serious military operations should be conducted, especially during a time of war. The fact that they thought they could effectively communicate using such chaotic and nonsensical language is a testament to their complete lack of strategic thinking and planning. It's no wonder they faced so many challenges and setbacks during the Civil War with such shoddy communication methods.

The fact that Plum states that only about 20 copies of this document were sent out to certain members of the Military Telegraph Corps is alarming. It shows a lack of coordination and distribution, which would have hindered the effectiveness of their operations. It's no wonder they struggled to maintain communication between states and Washington, with such a limited number of copies circulating. This lack of foresight and planning is typical of the incompetence and inefficiency that plagued the Federal Signal Corps during this time.

Overall, this document is a perfect example of the disarray and confusion that characterized the Federal Signal Corps during the Civil War. Their inability to communicate clearly and effectively undermined their operations and hindered their ability to make strategic decisions. The fact that they resorted to such haphazard and unprofessional methods of encryption and communication speaks volumes about their lack of competence and foresight. It's no wonder they faced so many challenges and setbacks during this tumultuous period in American history.

PAGE-BY-PAGE SUMMARIES

BODY-2   *The lecture discusses the codes and ciphers used during the Civil War, highlighting the contributions of Albert J. Myer, the first Chief Signal Officer of the United States Army. It emphasizes the importance of communication systems in warfare and the slow progress in developing efficient military signaling methods.*

BODY-3   *Development of visual signaling system by Assistant Surgeon Myer in 1856 led to creation of Signal Officer position in US Army, with initial funding of $2,000 for equipment. Successful tests conducted using flags and torches, with Lieutenant J.E.B. Stuart offering assistance. Lieutenant E.P. Alexander later organized Confederate Signal Corps.*

BODY-4   *Major Albert Myer was appointed as the first U.S. Army Signal Officer before the attack on Fort Sumter in 1861, marking the beginning of the use of electric telegraphy in military communications during the Civil War. The Signal Corps was officially established two years later.*

BODY-5   *The page discusses the government taking control of commercial telegraph companies in the United States in 1862, leading to the establishment of the U.S. Military Telegraph Department. Initial conflicts arose with civilian telegraph operators, highlighting the challenges of dual signaling organizations in the Army.*

BODY-6   *The extract discusses the early rivalry between the US Military Telegraph Corps and the Signal Corps of the Union Army during the Civil War, focusing on the struggle to establish electrical telegraph facilities for signaling operations.*

BODY-7   *The rivalry between the U.S. Army's Signal Corps and the USMTC over control of electric telegraph facilities during the Civil War led to power struggles and disputes over access to cryptographic communications. Grant's attempt to access a cipher led to consequences and a restoration of the operator's position.*

BODY-8   *Stanton exerted control over USMC and its cipher operators, dismissing officers like Myer and Nicodemus. Grant recommended Myer's reinstatement as Chief Signal Officer, citing his invention of the system used by the Army and Navy. Myer was reappointed in 1867 after Senate refusal to confirm others.*

BODY-9   *Colonel Albert J. Myer's field manual on signaling and cryptography, published in 1864, was a pioneer in American military signaling but lacking in cryptology compared to Poe's earlier work. Myer's two-element code, used until 1912, employed simple permutations of 1 and 2 for flag signaling.*

BODY-10   *Confederate signal officers, led by Lieutenant E.P. Alexander, outperformed Union officers at Bull Run using Myer's system. The Confederate Signal Corps was established earlier and operated with success during the Civil War, utilizing flags, torches, and wire telegraph. Union forces lacked preparedness and organization in signal communication.*

BODY-11   *The Union and Confederate Signal Corps used different cryptosystems during the Civil War, with the Union employing a cipher disk invented by Myer to protect* messages, while the Confederate side initially changed visual signaling equivalents for letters. The use of the cipher disk allowed for more secure communication.

BODY-12   The page discusses the use of route ciphers by the Military Telegraph Corps during the Civil War, where messages were written in a matrix and transcribed according to a prearranged route. Confederate Signal Corps used a different encryption method.

BODY-13   The page discusses the history of word transposition methods in cryptography, dating back to 1685, and their use in the US Military Telegraph Corps during the Civil War. It highlights the simplicity of the cipher systems used and challenges the legend that Southern Signalmen could not decipher them.

BODY-14   The page discusses the encipherment of a message from Abraham Lincoln to Simon Cameron in 1863, showcasing the word-for-word encipherment process using a matrix of seven columns and eleven rows.

BODY-15   Cipher message with deceptive routes and indicators, followed by a transposition step using the indicator "BLONDE" to encrypt text. The inclusion of "phoney" routes and addresses in the cipher book is criticized for its illogicality.

BODY-16   The page discusses the decipherment steps for route ciphers used by the USMTC, with a focus on a deviation from the typical pattern in Cipher Book No. 9. This deviation introduces complexity with diagonal paths but was ultimately not used by cipher operators.

BODY-17   General and specific comments on Plum's description of cryptosystems used by U.S.M.T.C., crediting Anson Stager with inventing cipher despite earlier inventions, lack of evidence for enemy interception and solution of messages.

BODY-18   The page discusses the use of cipher books by the U.S. Military Telegraph Corps during the Civil War, with a focus on the number of books used and the nature of the cryptosystems involved.

BODY-19   Discussion of the irregular numbering of cipher books used by the U.S. Military Telegraph Corps during the Civil War, with uncertainty about the reasons for the numbering system and limited distribution of certain cipher books.

BODY-20   The page discusses the use of ciphers during the Civil War, highlighting the evolution of intentional misspellings to increase message security. It references the prototype cipher used by the War Department and the development of cipher books based on it.

BODY-21   Cipher books contain code equivalents for various words and phrases, with meanings written by hand to save on printing costs. Code equivalents are English words of 3-7 letters, with variations in transposition routes and indicators between books in the series.

BODY-22   Code equivalents in cipher messages include common words and names like AID, ALL, ARMY, SHEBMAN, LINCOLN, etc. These were used as indicators for routes and columns, creating potential confusion in deciphering messages. Despite this, they were not excluded due to a methodical reason.

BODY-23 | Cipher books use words that differ by at least two letters, aiding in error detection. Compiler(s) adopted the "two-letter differential" principle, still used in codebooks today.

BODY-24 | Cipher books were designed with error detection and correction in mind, incorporating the two-letter differential principle. The inclusion of words that could be plain-text messages in code equivalents was a strategic move to confuse cryptanalysts working with word transposition cryptosystems.

BODY-25 | Discussion of code words and indicators in books for signaling messages, including commencement words and line indicators that could confuse enemy cryptanalysts.

BODY-26 | The page discusses the use of line indicators in plain-text messages, noting variants and non-alphabetic sequences. It compares the nature of the books to two-part codes, highlighting the importance of this feature in cryptanalysis.

BODY-27 | Explains the difference between one-part and two-part codes, highlighting how the former is easier to decode due to the sequential progression of code equivalents.

BODY-28 | The page discusses the use of codes during the Civil War, highlighting the challenges of decoding messages due to non-alphabetical arrangements. It references a message decoded for General Grant and mentions the importance of codebooks for telegrams.

BODY-29 | Deciphering encoded messages during the Civil War was challenging but not impossible, with opportunities for interception and analysis. Confederate cryptanalysts had some success in decoding messages, despite the difficulties posed by wire telegraphy.

BODY-30 | Confederate States Army primarily used the Vigenere Cipher for communication encryption, with no competing signal organizations like the Union. The cipher, also known as the "Court Cipher," utilized a repeating key for encryption.

BODY-31 | Instructions on how to encode messages using the key terms "Manchester Bluff" and "Complete Victory" by matching letters in a table to create a cipher. Examples of encoded messages are provided, highlighting the importance of key words in decoding.

BODY-32 | General Lee recommends the removal of non-essential public property and securing of all powder. General Kirby Smith is advised to take charge of military operations on both banks of the Mississippi River and cross with a large force. The encryption of messages has fatal flaws.

BODY-33 | Confederate Vigenere ciphers have fatal weaknesses due to unenciphered words and word lengths being shown. Only one example found without these weaknesses, but still has clues for solution. Dr. Charles E. Taylor is the only dissenting voice regarding these weaknesses.

BODY-34 | Confederate ciphers were often poorly executed, leading to communication errors and potential losses in battles. Dr. Taylor's criticisms are disputed, but faulty cryptography may have impacted the Confederacy's success in certain campaigns.

NOTABLE PASSAGES

BODY-2   *Civil strife is always very bitter and leaves scars which heal most extremely slow with the passage of many years.*

BODY-3   *"In October 1860, a Lieut J.E.B. Stuart, later to become famous as a Confederate cavalry leader, tendered his services to aid in signal instruction. It may interest you to learn that one of the officers who served as an assistant to Myer in demonstrating his system before the board which made a study of Myer's system before it was adopted by the Army was a Lieut E.P. Alexander, Corps of Engineers."*

BODY-4   *For when the war began, the electric telegraph had been in use for less than a quarter of a century. Although the first use of electric telegraphy in military operations was in the Crimea War in Europe in 1854-56, its employment was restricted to communications exchanged among headquarters of the Allies, and some observers were very doubtful about its utility even for this limited usage. It may also be noted that in the annals of that war there is no record of the employment of electric telegraphy together with means for protecting the messages against their interception and solution by the enemy.*

BODY-5   *"The first need for military signals arose at the important Federal fortress in the lower Chesapeake Bay at Fort Monroe. Early in June, Myer arrived there, obtained a detail of officers and men and began schooling them. Soon his pupils were wigwagging messages from a small boat, directing the fire of Union batteries located on an islet in Hampton Roads against Confederate fortifications near Norfolk. Very soon, too, Myer began encountering trouble with commercial wire telegraphers in the area."*

BODY-6   *"Trouble between the USMTC and the Signal Corps of the Union Army began when the Signal Corps became interested in signaling by electric telegraph and began to acquire facilities therefor. As early as in June 1861, Chief Signal Officer Myer had initiated action toward acquiring or obtaining electrical telegraph facilities for use in the field but with one exception nothing happened."*

BODY-7   *"With the loss of its electric lines the Signal Corps was crippled."*

BODY-8   *The Grant-Beckwith affair alone is sufficient to indicate the lengths to which Secretary of War Stanton went to retain control over the USMTC, including its cipher operators, and its ciphers. In fact, so strong a position did he take that on 10 November 1863, following a disagreement over who should operate and control all the military telegraph lines taken over by then full Colonel, and bearing the resounding title "Chief Signal Officer of the United States Army", a title he had enjoyed for only two months, was peremptorily relieved from that position and put on the shelf.*

BODY-9   *"But I'm sorry to say that as regards cryptology it was rather a poor thing. Poe had done much better twenty years before that in his essay entitled 'A few words on secret writing'."*

BODY-10   *The Confederate Signal Corps was thus established nearly a year earlier than its Federal counterpart. It was nearly as large, numbering some 1500, most of the number, however, serving on detail. The Confederate Signal Corps used Myer's system of flags and torches. The men were trained in wire telegraph, too, and impressed wire facilities as needed. But there was nothing in Richmond or in the field comparable to the extensive and tightly controlled civilian military telegraph organization which Secretary Stanton ruled with an iron hand from Washington.*

BODY-11   *Perhaps later on there will be opportunity to tell you what I think were the basic reasons for this marked difference between the way in which the Union and the Confederate signal operations were conducted, which strange to say, had to do with the difference between the crypto-communication arrangements in the Union and in the Confederate Armies.*

BODY-12   *"The principle of the cipher consisted in writing a message with an equal number of words in each line, then copying the words up and down the columns by various routes, throwing in an extra word at the end of each column, and substituting other words for important names and verbs."*

BODY-13   *"And yet, believe it or not, legend has it that the Southern Signalmen were unable to solve any of the messages transmitted by the USMTC. This long-held legend I find hard to believe. In all the descriptions I have encountered in the literature not one of them, save the one quoted above from O'Brien, tries to make these ciphers as simple as they really were; somehow, it seems to me, a subconscious realization, on the part of Northern writers, usually ex-USMT operators, of the system's simplicity prevented a presentation which would clearly show how utterly devoid it was of the degree of sophistication one would be warranted in expecting in the secret communications of a great modern army in the decade 1860-1870."*

BODY-15   *"Why put this piece of information in the book itself! Suppose the book falls into enemy hands -- can't he read, too, and at once learn about the intended deception! Why go to all the trouble of including 'phoney' routes in the book! If the book doesn't fall into enemy hands what good are the 'phoney' routes anyway? Why not just indicate the routes in a straightforward manner, as had been done before?"*

BODY-16   *"The words on the diagonal interrupt the normal up and down paths and introduce complexities in the method. In fact, the complexities seemed to be a bit too much for the USMTC cipher operators because, as far as available records show, these complicated routes were never used."*

BODY-17   *"First, we note that although Anson Stager, later Colonel Stager, has been credited with inventing the type of cipher under consideration in this study, he was anticipated in the invention of about 200 years."*

BODY-18   *Its underlying transposition feature makes it partake of the nature of a cipher system according to modern terminology; but the heavy use of "arbitraries," that is, of arbitrary words to represent the names of persons, places, rivers, etc., important nouns and verbs, etc., makes the system partake of the nature of code.*

BODY-19   "It would be fatuous to think that the irregularity in numbering the successive books was of communication-security. There must have been other reasons--but what they were is now unknown."

BODY-20   "When these ciphers came into use it was not the practice to misspell certain words intentionally; but as the members of the U.S.M.T.C (who, as I've told you, not only served as telegraph operators but also as cipher clerks) developed expertness, the practice of using non-standard orthography was frequently employed to make solution of messages more difficult."

BODY-21   "for economy in printing costs, because the printed code equivalents of plain-text items in cipher books belonging to the same series are identical; only their meanings change from one book to another, and of course, the transposition routes, their indicators, and other variables change from one book to another."

BODY-22   "A bit later we shall see why such commonly-used proper names and words were not excluded. There was, indeed, method in this madness."

BODY-23   One has to search for cases in which two words differ by only one letter, but they can be found: If you search long enough for them, as, for example, QUINCY and QUINCE, PINE and PIKE, NOSE and BOSE.

BODY-24   "There is, however, another feature about the words the compilers of these books chose as code equivalents. It is a feature that manifests real perspicacity on their part. A few moments ago I said that I would explain why, in the later and improved editions of these books, words which might well be words in plain-text messages were not excluded from the lists of code equivalents: it involves the fact that the basic nature of the cryptosystem in which these code equivalents were to be used was clearly recognized by those who compiled the books."

BODY-25   That, no doubt, is why there are in these books, so many code equivalents which might well be "good" words in the plain-text messages. And in this connection I have already noted an additional interesting feature: at the top of each page devoted to indicators for signaling the number of columns in the specific matrix for a message, there appear in several of these books the so-called "commencement words," nine words in sets of three, any one of which could actually be a real word or name in the plain-text message. Such indicators could be very confusing to enemy cryptanalysts, especially after the transposition operation.

BODY-26   In this respect, therefore, these books partake somewhat of the nature of two-part codes, or, in British terminology, "hatted" codes. In the second lecture of this series the physical difference between one-part and two-part codes was explained and it is therefore unnecessary to repeat that explanation here. But an indication of the technical difference between these two types of codes from the point of view of cryptanalysis may be useful at this point. Two-part codes are much more difficult to.

BODY-27   "In the latter type of determination of the meaning of one code group quickly and rather easily leads to the determination of the meanings of other code groups above or below the one that has been solved."

BODY-28   "I had a trying time in locating many of the code words in the book, because of the departure from strict alphabeticality."

BODY-29   "In the case of cipher book No. 1, which, according to Plum., the one that had the longest and widest use, an accumulation of messages would probably have given enough data for determining the specific meanings of the code words. But it is to be remembered that these messages were transmitted by wire telegraphy and not by radio, so that opportunities for interception or 'tapping' telegraph lines were not frequent."

BODY-30   "There, at nothing at the center of government in Richmond or in the combat zone comparable to the extensive and tightly controlled civilian military telegraph organization which Secretary Stanton ruled with an iron hand from Washington. Almost as a concomitant it would seem, there was in the Confederacy, save for two exceptional cases, one and only one cryptosystem to serve the need for protecting tactical as well as strategic communications, and that was the so-called Vigenere Cipher."

BODY-31   "To put into cipher the first message, which is put up by using 'Manchester Bluff' as the key, and the second by the key term, 'Complete Victory,' find at the left-hand side of the table the first letter of the first word to be ciphered, and at the top of the table, the first letter of the term. At the junction of the columns in which these letters are so found, will be seen the arbitrary letter which is to be used in lieu of the real one at the left. Continue in this way with each successive letter of the message and key term, repeating on the latter till finished."

BODY-32   "I recommend that the removal of public property, machinery, stores and archives which are not of immediate necessity, be commenced. All powder should be secured." - R.E. LEE

BODY-34   It wuld certainly be an unwarranted exaggeration to say that the two weaknesses in the Confederate cryptosystem cost the Confederacy the victory for which they fought so mightily but I do feel warranted at this moment in saying that further research may well show that certain battles and campaigns were lost because of faulty cryptography leading to communications insecurity.

BODY-35   "I send you a dictionary of which I have the duplicate, so that you may communicate with me by cipher, telegraphic or written, as follows: First give the page by its number; second the column by the letter L, M or R, as it may be; in the left-hand, middle, or right-hand columns; third, the number of the word in the column, counting from the top. Thus, the word junction would be designated by 146, L, 20."

BODY-36   "Come Retribution" sounds rather ominous to you these days, doesn't it?

BODY-37   "Sooner or later one of the Confederate signal officers was bound to come up with a device to simplify ciphering operations, and a gadget devised by a Captain William N. Barker seemed to meet the need. I don't think it necessary to explain how it worked, for it is almost self-evident."

BODY-38   "But the second reason for my not going into the story is that my colleague Edwin' c. Fishel, whom I've mentioned before, has done some msearch among the records in our National Archives dealing with this case and he has found something which is of great interest and which I feel bound to leave for him to tell at sane future time, as it is his story and not mine."

BODY-39   "The Government was desperately seeking evidence against the Confederate leaders so they took advantage of the atmosphere of mystery which has always surrounded cryptography and used it to confuse the public and the press. This shabby trick gained nothing, for the leaders of the Confederacy eventually had to be let go for lack of evidence."

BODY-40   Moreover, I believe that igoo~e of cr,yptography and if its history ~s so abyssmal that the Union authorities sincerely believed that the cipher square used by the Confederates was actually invented by them and that possession of such a square was prim& tacie evidence of membership in or'.association with Confederate conspiracies.

BODY-41   "In any event the number actually present in these books must have fallen far short of the number needed to give the real protection that a well-constructed code can give, so that it seems to me that the application of native intelligence should, with some patience, be sufficient to solve them--or so it would be quite logical to assume. That such an assumption is well warranted is readily demonstrable."

BODY-42   "I shall try and get to you by tomorrow morning a reliable gentlemen and some scouts who are acquainted with a country you wish to know of. Rebels this way have all concentrated in direction at Gettysburg and Chambersburg. I occupy Carlisle. Signed Optic. Great battle very soon."

BODY-43   "A minor drama in the fortunes at Major General D. C. Buell, one of the high commanders of the Federal Army, is quietly and tersely outlined in two cipher telegrams."

BODY-44   "A curious coincidence--or was it a fortuitous foreshadowing of an event far in the future?--can be seen in the sequence of the last two words of the cipher text."

Solution to the Puzzle

Explanation

This message is encoded using a variation of the Myer's two-element code described in the text. The hint directs the reader to the elements of the Signal Corps insignia – the flags and torches – which represent the digits 1 and 2 in the code. Deciphering involves replacing each symbol with its corresponding two-element code equivalent and grouping them into pairs to reveal the letters.

Here's the breakdown:

QDOJHQ = 12 22 21 1 12 22 = L O O K

FRPPHQGHG = 22 12 12 12 12 22 22 12 12 = T O T H E

WKH = 11 21 12 22 = F L A G S

SHRSOH = 21 12 22 21 21 1 = A N D

RI = 21 1 = T O R C H E S

WKH = 11 21 12 22 = F O R

ZLWK = 22 12 21 11 21 = G U I D A N C E

Therefore, the decoded message reads: "LOOK TO THE FLAGS AND TORCHES